RESPOND DON'T REACT

Close Encounters of the

Law Enforcement Kind

Vincent E. Green

G-Square Publishing

Department of Integrity

New York, New York

G-Square-Pub@optimum.net

G-SQUARE PUBLISHING

New York, New York

Department of Integrity

G-Square-Pub@optimum.net

Respond Don't React

Close Encounters of the Law Enforcement Kind

RESPOND DON'T REACT: Close Encounters of the Law Enforcement Kind

This book is designed to provide information with regard to the subject matter covered.

This information is shared with the understanding that neither the author nor G-Square Publishing is engaged in rendering legal or professional advice. Since the details of your situation are fact dependent, you should additionally seek the services of a competent professional.

Published by G-Square Publishing

888c 8th Avenue, New York NY 10019 USA

1.917.681.2810 | www.G-Square.org

G-Square Publishing is committed to excellence in the publishing industry. The organization reflects the philosophy established by the founders, based on its staunch belief in integrity, decency, and honor,

"Integrity has no equal."

Published in the United States of America

ISBN: 9781080400409

TABLE OF CONTENTS

ONE TO GROW ON

"If abuses are destroyed, man must destroy them.

If slaves are freed, mentally, and physically, man must free them.

If new truths are discovered, man must discover them.

If the naked are clothed.

If the hungry are fed.

If justice is done.

If labor is rewarded,

If superstition is driven from the mind.

If the defenseless are protected and if right finally triumphs,

All must be the work of man.

The grand victories of the future must be won by man, and by man alone."

Robert G. Ingersoll,

On the Gods and Other Essays

REASON FOR THIS PUBLICATIONS BEING

THIS PUBLICATION IS NOT INTENDED AS A DOCUMENT OF DIRECTION. ITS PURPOSE IS TO LEAD TO POSITIVE RESOLUTIONS WHEN ENCOUNTERING PROFESSIONAL MEMBERS OF LAW ENFORCEMENT.

The options shared in this work are merely those; options. Every situation is different. Each person is different. Therefore, how you and those involved will react or respond is likely to be different.

This publication provides food for thought with respect to the most appropriate course of action to take when encountering members of law enforcement.

The contents of this document have been reviewed and edited by career law enforcement personnel, attorneys, government officials, military officers, community activists, and educators, members of the clergy and young men and women who have had memorable encounters with law enforcement.

It is recognized that this sharing does not encompass the entire universe of options available to citizens, but they are a caring and thoughtful start.

We must each survive today, in the hope of sowing the seeds to hoe a path to ensure that tomorrow will harvest a better way.

It is my firm belief that absorbing this sharing will aid all parties involved in law enforcement encounters to resolve those encounters with professional law enforcement officers positively.

KNOW YOUR RIGHTS

DO YOU KNOW WHAT YOU THINK YOU KNOW?

1. Can a male officer search a female? _____

2. When arrested, must an individual be immediately read Miranda Warnings? _____

3. Is law enforcement allowed to lie during an interview or interrogation? _____

4. When do constitutional rights to counsel attach?
   _____

5. Who is your city council member or equivalent?
   _____

6. Who is your state senator or equivalent?
   _____

7. Who is your assemblyperson or equivalent?
   _____

8. Who is your lawyer versed in criminal matters?
   _____

1 SOMETIMES TRUTH CAN BE STRANGER THAN FICTION

"Where doth exist the antidote to indifference, more to the point, who among us is willing to swallow?"
Vinny Green

In 1951, Hollywood released the science fiction film, "The Day the Earth Stood Still." I was not even born at the time. The film was re-released in 2008[1]. In both renditions, aliens landed on the earth. The *reaction* of the citizens of earth to these alien beings, who clearly possessed a level of influence above that of most any resident of earth, was to *react* with earth's military presence against a force with which they were not familiar.

The earth force was not necessarily superior in tactical skills and had no true understanding of the tactics to employ to bring about a positive resolution to the encounter.

Earth's spontaneous *reaction* resulted in the destruction of the military force sent to face the aliens.

There were those among earth's *reaction* contingent who felt that a well-thought-out *response* to the alien presence was a superior plan of action. A plan, which was based on communication with the unfamiliar aliens was thought to be a far more prudent course of action. The execution of this

---

[1] https://www.imdb.com/title/tt0970416/

planned *response* resulted in the survival of the earth and its communities.

In 1977, Hollywood released another science fiction film. This one called "Close Encounters of the Third Kind." In this encounter with aliens, the residents of earth had presupposed the possibility of encountering aliens at some point in their lives and that those aliens might be in a better position to control the encounter than the communities of the earth would be.

The "What-If-Process"

Through the implementation of a series of "What-if" scenarios, which I believe is a lifesaving process to be employed by all and described in most of my writings, the individuals preparing for this encounter planned ahead and were ready with a plan of communication when, and if, this encounter took place.

This well-thought-out plan resulted in no need for military force when the encounter actually did take place, and more importantly, no loss of life or freedom.

The "What If Process" is critical in life and will be discussed in detail as we move through this publication. I implore you to embrace it because it sustains life.

I know that my readers are asking the question, why we are discussing sci-fi films in a work that should be presenting positive ways for interacting with law enforcement.

Take a breath, we will get there, but first, let us make sure that we have some understanding of "response vs. reaction." In addition, let us realize that in many respects, the Law Enforcement fraternity, of which I am a card-carrying member, can, from time to time, be seen to be made up of an alien force.

Close Encounters of the Law Enforcement Kind

Life's Encounters

While many of us give little to no thought on the subject, we each go through life experiencing at least three levels of encounters. The first encounter being that of family and friends. This encounter is usually a positive one, or at the very least, one in which we, as individuals, can take some control.

The second encounter is that one in which we encounter dealings with authority figures, such as teachers, clergy members, and bosses, to name just a few.

The third encounter being that of the *law enforcement kind*. An encounter that in a matter of moments, can change your very existence, if not, end it.

I have been a proud member, in good standing, of the law enforcement community for more than forty years. During my tenure, I have been able to achieve several admirable goals on behalf of the people. Each of those goals was achieved while in the alien role that I hold.

I have personally trained thousands of law enforcement officers in the United States, the African continent, and the Republic of Haiti. I have instilled in those men and women the importance of veracity and sincerity in all that they do as defenders of the people, all of the people.

I have gladly stood against corruption worldwide in the unique position of law enforcer for my entire adult life. I have every intention of continuing to do so as long as God allows breath in this body.

I can say with confidence that the vast majority of the men and women who have taken the singular and solemn oath as a law enforcement officer have done so with every intent on living up to that unique pledge in standing firm as a superior fighting force in protecting the people.

I can also say without fear of serious rebuttal that, yes, there are representatives of the law who have no real understanding of what that means. I pray each day that those officers will accept the injection of the vaccine of integrity, justice, and accountability.

Close Encounters of the Law Enforcement Kind

I have also been blessed by meeting and working with many people of honor and integrity of all races, creeds, and colors who have embraced this unique mission to protect the people; these were people of honor that I would enthusiastically stand side by side with as we faced the vicissitudes of life.

I have trained corruption fighters in the Republics of Haiti, Liberia, and Tanzania. I have lectured on the wickedness of corruption to United Nations Ambassadors and dignitaries from more than 75 countries.

I have held the position of Deputy Commissioner in the oldest corruption-fighting agency in existence. Most recently, I have held the position of Adjunct Professor in several colleges lecturing on the topics of ethics and the morality of man.

I have participated in all of these things with the full understanding that ours is a unique role, different from most any other that an individual may come upon. God has placed me here with a purpose, which I have absolutely no intention of questioning.

Through this more than forty-year trek, I have witnessed countless acts of failures to communicate, acts of discrimination, and undeserved hatred, leading to attempts at derailing what was hoped to be a well-planned life.

In each of these reactions and undeserved attacks, both big and small, I must admit that Friedrich Nietzsche was absolutely correct when he penned the words, "That which does not kill us, makes us stronger."

Each discriminatory act that I have witnessed or endured not only made me stronger but placed me in a mindset to make others stronger, as well.

2 CLOSE ENCOUNTERS

"Each man must be his own purveyor of truth."
Vinny Green

The focus of this publication is to educate the reader on some of the most appropriate ways to safely and successfully interact with professional members of law enforcement.

Make no mistake, close encounters with law enforcement can seem alien to most of us on the receiving end of the encounter. In fact, such an encounter can work as if a lifelong infection in the life of most anyone encountering a law enforcement representative.

Such an encounter can leave a harsh memory and a feeling of trauma like no other kind. While most of us, or maybe none of us, except for me, give it any thought, it must be understood that being a law enforcement officer requires the individual empowered with the authority to uphold the law to very often find themselves in the role of a changeling.

Some enforcers at the very least must be able to be an individual capable of morphing into sometimes a completely different being in order to make it from one day to the next.

For some, being a law enforcement officer requires the officer to become an alien of the law enforcement kind. Actually, that may well contribute to the perceived problem.

Strapping on that suit of armor, which most of us call a uniform, or

Close Encounters of the Law Enforcement Kind

displaying that shield of authority, which we call a badge, in many instances changes my barbequing neighbor next door, into an alien with the perception that only he knows right from wrong. That the suit of armor and the shield of, *I know best*, somehow endows him with superior know-how; I have seen it. I have sat across the table from it. Hell, there may even be some that will say; Tag, you're it! I pray that is not the case, but I have worn rose-colored glasses more than once in my life.

My Encounter in this Alien World

I grew up in the "Projects," at least that is what my neighborhood and those like it were called. These days they are called "Developments" in what I think is a useless effort to remove the stigma of the title of "Projects." In truth, the stigma remains, despite the name. A rose by any other name…

The distinction is that despite the labeling process and inaccurate assumptions that seem to go on that the Projects have always been the home to the underclass, made up predominately of people of color. The truth is that my project, like many others, was not inhabited predominately by people of color. People of color were the clear minorities in the development in which I lived.

I was born and raised in the Bayview Housing development, managed by the New York City Housing Authority. To me, it was an oasis, building young men and women destined for various levels of greatness, whatever greatness may be.

Growing up, I interacted with law enforcement on a regular basis. In the projects, there was a small contingent of police officers assigned solely to protect our development.

As a youth, my encounters with the project law enforcement officers consisted of the officers making sure we did not play on the grass, ride our bikes in undesignated areas, and that we did not make a lot of noise.

Close Encounters of the Law Enforcement Kind

I remember Officer Jenkins, an African American Officer who patrolled the grounds and knew us all by name. If you broke the rules, Jenkins rarely chased you, unless it was some extremely serious infraction or crime, but when you got home, he would be in your Livingroom talking with your dad, and sometimes maybe even having a beer.

Whatever discipline was required would be dispensed by dad, right then and there. This response was pretty much the same with the other officers in the development as well, but none more than Officer Jenkins.

As it happened, Jenkins was also the Officer respected more than any other. Actually, we all respected law enforcement because of the relationships that had been established, which in most instances, seemed fair.

There were even Police Officers living in the development. I remember Officer Allen, a police officer whose children were close friends with my oldest brother and sister. He and his wife would play cards with my parents on Saturday night.

We even had a ground breaking female as a Bayview inhabitant. Ruth, a close family friend, was a proud member of the force. She was a detective in the police department, one of the first females and African Americans to hold such a position. Her husband Joe was also a member of the force. I remember being impressed at the fact that she conducted undercover operations. It inspired me to do the same when I entered the profession.

Jerry Morgan held a management position in the police department; he oversaw keeping the peace in several housing developments in Brooklyn, including Bayview (the View), he was especially good at his profession. When he passed away at an early age, he was promoted posthumously to the rank of Captain.

Captain Morgan's wife was my mom's best friend, and my second mother, his son has been my lifelong friend. Captain Morgan was not a drinking man or card player, like many of the Bayview inhabitants, but he was a true friend until the end.

Close Encounters of the Law Enforcement Kind

I never experienced anything negative growing up in the View by the hands of the Officers assigned to watch over us kids. That is not to say that I was pleased with all of the actions taken by the officers in the development. As I reflect on my youth, I have to admit I cannot point to a situation where their actions were not, for lack of a better term, fair.

However, as I grew, and ventured out of the View, my interaction with many of the men in blue took the direction of a negative view. In the early stages, it was not a situation of any kind of abuse, but I began to see an elitist attitude and an entitlement view that I never knowingly witnessed before.

I remember several families from the "the View" going on a cookout at a state park in Up State New York. Officer Allen and members of his family were there as well. He was riding in the car with my family, and my dad was driving. As we exited the Belt Parkway, which is where our development began, my dad was pulled over by a cop and asked for his license and registration.

I could not have been more than ten or eleven-years-old. I do not know why we were pulled over; in fact, I am not sure if my dad knew either. I say this because Officer Allen immediately displayed his shield to the Officer who stopped us, and with little further conversation, the officer sent us on our way. There was no indication that the stopping Officer knew Officer Allen in any way other than having a badge in his pocket.

I am not prepared to say if the Officer that sent us on our way was right or wrong, because I do not know why we were stopped. What I do know is that if not for Officer Allen being in the car that day, there is a good chance that it could have turned out in a different way.

That was one of my first experiences of seeing that a fraternal mindset existed in this alien organization. Again, not saying that it was wrong, just saying that it was. I can say that fifty years have come and gone, and the incident is still fresh in my mind as if I were still eleven years old. I do not believe that alien encounters fade away.

Close Encounters of the Law Enforcement Kind

Even as a young boy, it left me wondering about being a part of an organization that should be held to high standards of ethical operation and if that were possible. In fact, those thoughts traveled with me for my entire career and still do, to this day. This day was not the last time that I witnessed what appeared to be a benefit bestowed by one officer upon another.

Honoring the Team

In the ninth grade, I entered Canarsie High school. It was there that I joined the Junior Varsity Football Team. As the school year ended, I remember Coach Yaker, who was the head of the Junior Varsity football team giving us our team jersey and tee shirts.

Coach Yaker gave a clear and powerful directive that we now represented the Canarsie Chief's Football team, and we were to do nothing that would bring dishonor or shame to that name. I wore those garments with enormous pride.

I was fifteen at the time. I remember on one particularly hot day in the View; I was in what we called "The Big Park," playing handball. Three plainclothes police officers entered the park with a Caucasian man that I knew to be from the neighborhood.

One of the officers acted as if he wanted to play handball, which was a silly rouse because all of us knew who they were. While they were not a part of the Project law enforcement team, we knew they were assigned to the 69th precinct, which covered Canarsie, of which Bayview was a part.

We all stopped playing because we knew something bad was about to happen. One of the officers walked up to me with the resident and pointed to me and said, was it him? The resident said, yes, and the officer placed me in handcuffs and said, I was under arrest.

Even now, some forty-five years later, I can hear the handcuffs cinched up on my wrist. At the age of fifteen, I had never known the level of fear and confusion; I was feeling at that moment. I had no idea what was

Close Encounters of the Law Enforcement Kind

going on. My parents were at a wedding, and I was unable to reach them.

There were no cellphones in those days. After being told why I was arrested, which included an absurd charge of kidnapping and several other charges that I no longer recall, but to this day, I can still hear the detective saying the word, "kidnapping," I repeatedly tried to explain that the resident was wrong, and he had made a mistake. In fact, during the time that he claimed I committed the crime in question, I was home watching a New York Jets football game with family and friends.

My relentless pleas to be heard and believed did nothing to stop the officers from continuing to process my arrest. An accusation had been made and a finger pointed in my direction. That accusation did not come with an opportunity for me to be heard, before officially documenting an event that would follow me for the rest of my life.

I sat handcuffed to a chair in the precinct. There was no effort made to contact my parents or anyone who could act in my best interest. After about three hours of being in that chair, again with no opportunity to be heard, Captain Morgan walked into the room and directed the cuffs to be removed. He had been contacted by one of the kids in the park that witnessed the event. He then confirmed that I was, in fact, at home during the time that I was accused of committing the crime and that he was there watching the game as well. For the record, the Captain's statement was true.

I was released, not with an apology, but the arresting officer told me that I could go home and that I should thank the Captain. This to me suggested that my pleas of innocence were not necessarily believed, but that my release was based on a member of the fraternity stepping up to speak on my behalf. I assume that some other discussion took place that warranted my release other than just Captain Morgan's word. I do not know what that discussion was.

At the time, that was more than enough for me. As I walked out of the precinct, I walked by a mirror, and I felt tears welling up in my eyes, not because of what had taken place, as traumatizing as it was, but it was at that point that I realized that I was wearing my Canarsie Chief's football tee-shirt.

Close Encounters of the Law Enforcement Kind

While the entire incident was a case of mistaken identity, it did not matter; any one seeing me in that shirt would only know that a Canarsie Chief was taken away in handcuffs. I had dishonored the team. All I could hear was Coach Yaker's voice on the last day of practice admonishing us to always bring honor to the team.

The next day, the individuals that actually committed the crime were arrested. I saw the resident several times after the incident. Sadly, an apology never rolled from his lips. I was told that he offered the explanation to the arresting officer that I looked like one of the guys in question. As I understood it, they were all in their twenties with facial hair. Again, I was fifteen with only the hair on my head and the beginnings of pubic hair. What it came down to in that resident's mind was that once again, we all look alike.

Before leaving the precinct, I was told that the record of my arrest would be expunged. At the age of fifteen, I really did not know what that meant or why it would matter to me.

When I applied for my first position in law enforcement, why it mattered came screaming at me. As it turns out, the record was expunged, but that did not apply when seeking any law enforcement position. That day of dishonor came up in my background investigation, and I had to explain what happened on that day.

In fact, over the years, I have received at least ten promotions or applied for law enforcement positions, and in each case, I had to explain that close encounter with law enforcement, no matter the fact that I had done nothing wrong.

This incident is something I share with any youth groups with whom I am honored to speak. They need to know that their close encounters can and will change their lives. I strongly recommend to them all to do all that they can to legally avoid such close encounters.

3 A MEMBER OF THE FRATERNITY

"While stupidity is a given, human beings need to be saved from ignorance."
Vinny Green

I must admit that my negative encounters with law enforcement have been few. Having said that, I could not say how many encounters it takes to change your life forever. I could not write with a straight face that my limited encounters were due to me doing everything right. I believe that a lot of it has to do with two factors, one being that I am a member of the law enforcement fraternity and have a much better sense of simple acts that may draw the attention of a law enforcement officer in a negative way.

The other being that I have been a trainer of law enforcement officers for more than three decades. I know what I have taught officers with respect to what to avoid and what to be concerned about.

Just to be clear, this does not mean that I have never been pulled over. I must admit that the few times I have been stopped, to me, they were humiliating experiences.

One encounter particularly stands out in my memory. I was leaving my old neighborhood in the View, after visiting my sister. I was in my mini-van along with my wife, daughter, and grandson. As I turned off Rockaway Parkway to enter the Belt Parkway, several unmarked police cars, lights flashing, and a blaring siren, pulled up behind us. Several plainclothes officers leaped out of the vehicle with guns drawn.

19

Close Encounters of the Law Enforcement Kind

As I mentioned earlier, I am a big believer in the What If Process. In employing WIP, I always take myself through possible negative encounters in life and go through in my mind how I would respond to such encounters.

My law enforcement WIP for driving encounters always includes as one of my first steps to place any type of parking permit on the dashboard of the vehicle I am driving that I might have. Such an action will usually initiate civil discussion between myself and the law enforcement professional.

Civil conversation is your first defense in most any potential negative encounter, I recognize that we do not all have the luxury of placing a permit or conversation starter on our dashboards, which is why my WIP defensive strategy also includes encounters where this particular strategy is not an option.

My initial WIP is intended to alert an officer stopping me that I am a law-abiding citizen that understands the concept of rules and procedures. Think about it, in obtaining any document to be displayed in your vehicle usually requires the filing of paperwork and the following of rules. Having the officer with this mindset about who you are is a good place to start any encounter.

This tactic helps to de-escalate any negative emotions that might be brewing or already in play. It might not stop it, but it will give it pause, and that is a good thing because it allows for the de-escalation of negative emotions that may be forming. In the incident that was unfolding, I assumed that guns drawn suggested negative emotions were in play.

However, before reaching my vehicle, and totally contrary to any training that I have ever given a law enforcement officer, all of the officers began screaming orders.

Multiple officers talking at the same time is a very dangerous tactic on the part of the officers in that the individual being given the orders has no idea whom to obey.

Close Encounters of the Law Enforcement Kind

Having trained, and mentally prepared for this situation over the years, I employed what I call the "Gift of Gab," the all-important powerful tactic of communication. I also made sure that my hands were visible throughout the encounter to avoid the officers experiencing any feelings of being threatened.

As they approached my vehicle with guns drawn, one of them saw my permit in the window and asked if I was on the job. Even though I am not a member of the police department, at the time, I was a member of law enforcement in the City's anti-corruption department with full law enforcement authority.

I responded that I was on the job for no other reason than to convey a level of comfort. If I had to explain further, I would have been more than happy to do that once I felt that all parties involved felt comfortable with one another. I did not want my family exposed to any further humiliation or danger than they were already experiencing.

I advised the officers that my shield was in my pocket and asked for permission to retrieve it, which one of them consented to. When I took out my badge, and they saw stars on the badge, which is a symbol of authority within many law enforcement agencies; each of the officers immediately became apologetic. At that point, I was not so much interested in apologies as I was in removing my family from this unfriendly encounter.

If not for WIP, in addition to having my permit, understanding law enforcement training and having my shield, this encounter could have gone horribly different. The encounter took place more than fifteen years ago, my grandson was not even a teenager at the time, but he still remembers the encounter, just as I remember my encounter at the age of eleven, not cool.

Minor interactions can have life-long impacts

Anyone of the negative encounters that I have shared, which rolled out in my life, could have had disastrous effects on my life and derailed who I was able to grow up to be. Something such as "Stop and Frisk" or even

Close Encounters of the Law Enforcement Kind

unpaid parking tickets, which cannot always be timely paid by some of the less fortunate members of society, can result in jail time or in some states suspension of revenue-generating drivers' licenses, could begin a downward spiral in life. Much of it begins with our youth, and in many cases, adults reacting to law enforcement, instead of responding to that force.

It is time for a frank discussion on survival tactics, be you black, brown, white, yellow or, red working to navigate law enforcement's impregnable gates. If for some insane reason, there are those in this society who believe that color is the determining factor in our societal woes, please explain how that goes.

At what point does pigmentation decide which way one will go? What is the shade of skin that determines at what level a person will sin? If you foolishly think it is all about economics, the simple solution would be, level the playing field; no need for handouts, just opportunities to step up. If you think it is a matter of intellect, then invest in education, instead of mass incarceration.

The bottom line is that you cannot fix the perceived problem by locking it away. It is well past time to shine the bright light of integrity and decency into the mirrors in which we daily see. It is there that we, as a people, and I mean human beings, will see the reflection and cause of all the ills that have infected the body politic. We must each remove the beam from our eyes so that we may obtain untrammeled vision when we look upon our brothers and sisters.

Yes, the illnesses known as hate and segregation can be cured, all we need do is release the floodgates of caring, lift the downtrodden from the rocky depths of polluted waters and spend each day of our lives doing just one thing to make life better. I guarantee you; it will become contagious in a life-sustaining way. As the song goes; each man is my brother; each man is my friend[2].

---

[2]

https://www.lyricsfreak.com/j/joan+baez/no+man+is+an+island_20493107.html

4 JUST THE FACTS

"Each man must be his own purveyor of truth."
Vinny Green

The focus of this publication is to educate the reader on some of the most appropriate ways to safely and successfully interact with professional members of law enforcement. Before doing so, I would like to share a few facts with respect to the criminal justice system in the United States and those members of society being incarcerated within that system in alarmingly large percentages.

A more detailed discussion on Mass Incarceration can be found in the upcoming G-Square publication entitled: *I weep for the Nation that Rebukes Integration in Favor of Mass Incarceration.*

I fully understand that readers of this work may have differing points of view as to contributions made by African Americans, Hispanics, Latinos, and other citizens of color to the crime rate in the United States. In fact, my research on this subject has presented a bevy of differing points of view.

To adequately address the question; assuming that it even needs to be addressed as part of this work; would require multiple chapters focusing solely on the question of, who is the cause of crime in this great nation?

In the interest of moving to the actual subject matter of this undertaking, I provide the following information as food for thought and truth. The Federal Bureau of Investigation crime statistics for 2016 reports the information in the below charts[3].

TOTAL ARREST BY RACE[4]

RACE	ARRESTS
WHITE	5,858,330
BLACK OR AFRICAN AMERICAN	2,263,112
AMERICAN INDIAN OR ALASKAN NATIVE	171,185
ASIAN	103,244
NATIVE HAWAIIAN OR OTHER PACIFIC ISLANDER	25,610
TOTAL	8,421,481

[3]https://ucr.fbi.gov/crime-in-the-u.s/2016/crime-in-the-u.s.-2016/topic-pages/tables/table-21
[4] Hispanic and Latino are usually defined as an ethnicity, as opposed to a race.

PERCENTAGE DISTRIBUTION

RACE	PERCENTAGE
WHITE	69.6
BLACK OR AFRICAN AMERICAN	26.9
AMERICAN INDIAN OR ALASKAN NATIVE	2.0
ASIAN	1.2
NATIVE HAWAIIAN OR OTHER PACIFIC ISLANDER	0.3
TOTAL	100%

OVERVIEW

Arrests, by Race and Ethnicity, 2016[5]

- In 2016, 69.6 percent of all individuals arrested were White, 26.9 percent were Black or African American, and 3.6 percent were of other races.
- Of arrestees for whom ethnicity was reported, 18.4 percent were Hispanic or Latino.
- Of all juveniles (persons under the age of 18) arrested in 2016, 62.1 percent were White, 34.7 percent were Black or African American, and 3.2 percent were of other races.
- Of all adults arrested in 2016, 70.2 percent were White, 26.2 percent were Black or African American, and 3.6 percent were of other races.
- White individuals were arrested more often for violent crimes than individuals of any other race and accounted for 59.0 percent of those arrests.
- White juveniles accounted for 58.4 percent of all juveniles arrested for property crimes.

---

[5]https://ucr.fbi.gov/crime-in-the-u.s/2016/crime-in-the-u.s.-2016/topic-pages/tables/table-21

➢ Of juveniles arrested for drug abuse violations, 74.8 percent were White.

The first point I would like to emphasize on this matter is this; I have always been told that numbers do not lie; people lie. If we are looking at the numbers as presented, as well as, percentages, the lesson to learn and apply is this; the numbers show that the premier crime-fighting agency in the nation clearly states that African Americans and Hispanic or Latinos have not earned the distinction as the race or ethnic leaders in committing crime.

Any effort to skew these numbers by percentages, self-serving charts, geographical breakdowns, full moons, or tarot cards, will not support a claim that blacks or Hispanics are the leading cause of crime in this nation.

My second point on the topic is this; I have been Black my entire life, and I have never committed a crime, be it violent, drug-related or otherwise; therein ends the lesson.

This Great Nation

Today, the United States makes up approximately 5 percent of the world's population. Unfortunately, the U.S., one of the most advanced and wealthiest nations on the face of the earth, also gets to claim 21 percent of the world's incarcerated population[6].

The United States of America is one of the few countries in existence that still maintains the practice of invoking the death penalty on its citizens. The number of American citizens with criminal records is approximately equal to that of Americans with a 4-year college degree[7].

Recent studies have shown that 1 in every 37 adults in the United States, or 2.7 percent of the adult population, is under some form of correctional supervision. Those forms include prison, jail, parole, or

---

[6] http://www.naacp.org/criminal-justice-fact-sheet/
[7] http://www.naacp.org/wp-content/uploads/2017/06/FCH-Fact-sheet-rev.-5-5-17.pdf

probation.

In addition, approximately half of African American males and nearly 40 percent of white males end up arrested by the time they reach the age of 23[8]. As of 2007, more than half of the inmates in United States correctional facilities were parents of children under the age of 18[9]. These are not statistics upon which strong family units are built.

Racial Disparities in Incarceration

In the 2015, US Census, it is estimated that 46,282,080 African Americans live in the United States. This number tells us that 14.3 percent of the total American population of 321.4 million are Black people[10].

In 2014, African Americans, not all people of color, constituted 2.3 million, or 34 percent, of the total 6.8 million correctional population[11]. This number is six times greater than the number of slaves who were kidnapped and ultimately marooned in this nation.

African Americans are incarcerated at more than five times the rate of white Americans. The incarceration rate for African American women is twice that of white women[12].

Established Facts

Though Blacks and Hispanics comprise 32 percent of the population in the United States, in 2015, they constituted 56 percent of all incarcerated people.

If Blacks and Hispanics were incarcerated at similar rates as whites,

---

[8] https://www.naacp.org/criminal-justice-fact-sheet/
[9] https://bjs.gov/content/pub/pdf/pptmc.pdf
[10] http://www.ctsfw.net/media/pdfs/GrayServingJesusatChurch.pdf
[11] http://www.naacp.org/criminal-justice-fact-sheet/
[12] ibid

prison and jail populations would decline by almost 40 percent, leading to the significant and immediate availability of resources for investing in such admirable goals as better schools, housing, and healthcare[13].

Nationwide, African American youth represent 32 percent of children who are arrested, 42 percent of children who are detained, and 52 percent of children whose cases are judicially waived to criminal court[14], meaning these children are incarcerated with adults, where there will be a percentage of career criminals looking to expand their criminal empires[15].

These sentencings do nothing more than place African American youth into an abusive criminal training academy, not a rehabilitation facility. Herein extends the cycle of mass incarceration.

---

[13] http://www.naacp.org/criminal-justice-fact-sheet/
[14] http://www.naacp.org/criminal-justice-fact-sheet/
[15] https://www.naacp.org/criminal-justice-fact-sheet/

5 NURTURE THE SEED

"Reacting is a powerful choice in life, but it is responding that demonstrates honor, accountability, good character, and integrity."
Vinny Green

This publication is intended to plant a seed of contemplation, which we pray will take root as each of us goes about our daily interaction with the more than 1.1 million persons employed on a full-time basis, nationwide in the myriad of law enforcement agencies established in our communities. This number includes 765,000 sworn full-time law enforcement personnel; any one of whom you may encounter in the ordinary course of your day.

A recent census has documented that nationwide, law enforcement organizations also employ approximately 100,000 part-time employees, including 44,000 sworn officers[16].

Many of us may never have a need to encounter a law enforcement official, be it positive or negative. However, given these numbers, there is a high likelihood that you will, in fact, interact with a law enforcement official at some point in your life.

Within these words, there is no conscious attempt or intent to cast an ominous shadow upon the eye of integrity that is the center of the storm that law enforcement walks in each day as they work to carry out the mission of protecting and serving the people of this nation. We pledge

---

[16] https://www.bjs.gov/content/pub/pdf/csllea08.pdf

support to those men and women who put their lives on the line to safeguard our freedoms.

Within any civilized society, there will be a need for honest, efficient, respectful, and ethics-based law enforcement. There is no more noble profession in any society formed by man, than serving the people.

There is no greater human responsibility or undertaking than civil, thoughtful, and unbiased enforcement of the laws of the land. With the establishment of such enforcement organizations, which will be staffed by imperfect Human Beings, we have a responsibility and duty to ensure that, "We, the people," do the utmost to respect those enforcing the law.

However, it is equally important to understand our rights and responsibilities as we interact with the men and women, we charge with the responsibility to uphold those laws and protect our very existence.

If you take away nothing else from this publication, please understand this; Nothing in Life Happens in a Vacuum. What you say, what you do, and yes, even what you think, will have an impact on someone else, despite what your intent may be.

Even if you decide to toss this document into the next trashcan that you see, recognize that the tossing you chose to engage in, is a result of these words making you think about the feelings and ideas that have been put before you.

It does not matter if you believe what has been expressed in these lines. What does matter is that words have influence. With few exceptions, well-intentioned people do not go through life firing words indiscriminately.

As I have written in other publications, in fact, quoting my father, "Language is a poor form of communication, but it is all that we have right now." While you may speak the same language as those you encounter, including law enforcement, you do not always hear the same message.

The factor that makes each of us able to communicate is not so much a common language, but more so, common experiences and the daily usage of the language.

Close Encounters of the Law Enforcement Kind

Some of us speak the same language and still have difficulty communicating with one another, mainly because of different experiences in life, values, and culture.

In an effort to communicate, you do not begin on a level language playing field. If you think about it, you will find that people usually have to dig out of a communication ditch to receive the message and then interpret the message.

The interpretation must focus on the difference between speech and comprehension, the difference between understanding the words, and understanding the meaning.

This lack of certainty in communication means we must always use care in our methods of communication, especially when interacting with law enforcement and others of authority.

6 WHEN APPROACHED, RESPOND, DO NOT REACT

"It is the relentless enemy within that stifles the growth of men."
Vinny Green

Reactions are usually instinctive and may be well suited for battle. However, Responses are more often reasoned and planned and therefore, likely to be more appropriate for encounters with law enforcement.

There are lifesaving and straightforward steps that we all need to be aware of and try our best to use to our advantage. The following recommendations are presented with the intent of providing a safe path home with no detours that will require my readers and listeners to become tangibly versed in the ways of the criminal justice system.

In this publication, we are hoping to provide you with useful information and strategies to avoid arrest, harm, or other negative encounters with law enforcement.

Some knowledge is better absorbed by reading or lecture, than experiencing firsthand. An understanding of the criminal justice system is such a case.

I implore you to recognize and understand that a close encounter with the criminal justice system is a real possibility in all of our lives. The only requirement is that you be alive.

Close Encounters of the Law Enforcement Kind

Given that this encounter is highly likely, each of us has a responsibility to give thought to our response to this inevitable event now, rather than reacting to it cold when confronted by it unprepared.

In all of the training manuals, books, and presentations prepared by the G-Square International Training Academy, or G-Square Publishing, ample discussion focuses on the idea of preparing for the possibility of things going wrong on any given day.

What I am talking about once again, is WIP. My friends, WIP is not rocket science; it is just a common-sense approach to survival and walking through life, day by day.

What WIP simply says is that it would be foolish to wait for a situation to unfold in front of us, and then try to prepare a plan of action on the fly. Because of the conditions in which we currently live, we must engage the WIP mindset once the good Lord allows our eyes to open and we are in our right minds.

For each of us, it is at that point in which we must begin thinking about how to sensibly and lawfully respond to situations such as an encounter with law enforcement. This encounter includes something as mundane as driving in heavy traffic, which, unbelievably, could end in a law enforcement encounter, and for many people can be the beginning of the end of life as they have known it and dreamt it to be.

If we wait until it happens, it is far too late to think about an effective, lawful, and successful response. As a result, we are reduced to a scattershot reaction resulting in a path taken that can ultimately misdirect our lives.

I encourage you to consider the following as part of your law enforcement WIP. If this does not work for you, then delete it from your mind, but not before contemplating an alternate sensible response:

1. Stay calm and remember that words do not come attached to a fishhook and line, allowing you to reel them back in.
2. If you must speak, choose your words wisely.

Close Encounters of the Law Enforcement Kind

3. Never forget that your body language and emotions say far more than your oral speak.
4. When speaking to law enforcement, do not use your hands and arms in an effort to emphasize the point you are trying to make. These actions can be easily misinterpreted and seen as a hostile act.
5. Keep your hands at your side or visibly in the air if directed to do so. In all of this, maintain a non-threatening posture.
6. Choose words that will de-escalate the encounter, not escalate into a negative confrontation.
7. Avoid being or appearing hostile.
8. Avoid making the encounter with law enforcement a negative confrontation.
9. Make every effort to maintain a civil and professional demeanor.
10. It is recommended that you comply with lawful instructions.
11. Remember, anything you say or do will most likely be used against you, so if there is no need to talk, shut up.
12. Do not attempt to flee from the encounter.
13. Avoid touching any law enforcement officer.
14. Innocent or not, do not engage in physical or verbal resistance.
15. If you complain at the scene or tell law enforcement, they are wrong, do so in a non-hostile way that will not escalate tensions that may exist or be forming.
16. To some, these may seem like steps toward surrendering in some way; maybe it is, but if you are not in control, hold your tongue and the dynamic changes in your favor.
17. Recognize that being right does not place you in control.
18. It is recommended that you do not make or write any statements regarding the incident without advice from competent legal criminal counsel.
19. Remember the names of officers on the scene, badge numbers, patrol car numbers, and physical descriptions. It is easier to remember numbers two digits at a time.
20. Write everything down as soon as possible.
21. Before the encounter begins or is about to start, if conditions allow for placing a call on your cell phone, do so to enable others to hear the encounter.
22. If conditions allow for it, activate the record feature on your cell phone or other electronic devices.

Close Encounters of the Law Enforcement Kind

23. If eyewitnesses gather around the scene during your encounter with law enforcement officers, speak clearly enough for the witnesses to overhear what is going on and what is said during the encounter, and refrain from using abusive language or language that can be interpreted as hostile or threatening.
24. Request witnesses to take pictures or video of the encounter.
25. Find witnesses and obtain their contact information.
26. If you are injured, seek medical attention no matter how minor.
27. Make sure medical personnel attending to your injuries are aware that the injuries are the result of a law enforcement encounter.
28. Have photographs taken of the injury.
29. Obtain copies of the medical report.
30. If the situation calls for it, you or someone on your behalf should file a law enforcement Misconduct Complaint as soon as possible.

7 PUT YOUR PRIDE IN CHECK AND EXECUTE A RESPONSE

"It is in the eye of the storm where peace resides."
Vinny Green

In preparing your WIP, it is suggested that you consider the following in your plan of action:

1. Consider limiting your conversation to only pedigree information[17].
2. Remember that whatever you say, you will likely hear again, and it is possible your words will be used against you.
3. Consider the fact that your initial encounter will most likely be the first in a series of encounters that will be taking place as you move through the criminal justice process.
4. Your words and actions will be a contributing factor in determining how well things go in your favor.
5. Immediately advise the officer that you would like to exercise your right to remain silent, and then, seriously consider doing so.
6. If others are arrested with you, consider **recommending** to them in a non-hostile and non-interfering way, not to make any statements and to remain silent unless told to do otherwise by competent legal criminal counsel.
7. It is not recommended that you try to force these individuals into remaining silent. Their rights are not for you to exercise for them.
8. Exercising this right on your behalf, protects *your* Fifth Amendment Constitutional Rights, also known as Miranda Warnings.

---

[17] While in custody, an officer is likely to ask for what is called "pedigree" information. Pedigree information is the type of information that it is usually in your best interest to share, such things as your name, address, and date of birth. However, this is your decision to make.

Close Encounters of the Law Enforcement Kind

9. When possible, address the officer by name, such as Officer Jones, most officers wear a nametag. You might not like the situation, but you must always seek to control the situation. Common courtesy will help get you there.
10. Respect the position, if not the person.
11. You need not consent to a search of yourself, your belongings, your vehicle, or your home[18]. However, if the Officer insists on a search, it is recommended that you not resist, but that you make it clear that you are not granting permission. It is not likely that resisting will go well for you.
12. If the Officer says he has a warrant, ask to see it.
13. Check the warrant for accuracy.
14. If you detect any inaccuracies in the warrant, point them out in a professional, non-hostile manner.
15. Do not lose control because you think you have an "I gotcha" moment.
16. If the warrant is not produced, it is recommended that you clearly communicate to the Officer, "I do not consent to this search." Clearly stating your refusal to give consent protects your Fourth Amendment Right against unreasonable search and seizure.
17. Verbally and in a non-hostile manner refusing a search is not grounds for arrest. However, physically trying to resist the search can, and probably will result in arrest.
18. This refusal may not stop the search from happening, but it will protect your rights should the encounter end up in a criminal proceeding.
19. It is recommended that you not entertain any offers presented to you as so-called deals, which will "disappear if you do not agree immediately."
20. State your desire to have a criminal attorney present before any questioning takes place or offers are made.
21. If there is a deal to be made, it will likely require the consent of a prosecutor.
22. Allow your criminal attorney to negotiate with the State's attorney. Assuming he or she is competent, your attorney will be the best at negotiating any deals that are to be had.

---

[18] Please keep in mind, if the officer has a warrant, consent is no longer a factor; you should comply with the lawful search.

Close Encounters of the Law Enforcement Kind

23. When being questioned by law enforcement, it is your Fifth Amendment rights that will best serve you. Miranda warnings offer you the right to remain silent, consider exercising that right.

24. While you can request an attorney, your Sixth Amendment right to have an attorney present does not attach until, what the Supreme Court has defined as a significant or critical stage in a criminal proceeding. In a criminal setting, it is commonly known that the accused has a legal right to be represented by an attorney. However, it is probably not as well known that the right to an attorney is limited and only exists during certain phases of a criminal proceeding called "critical stages."[19]

25. Do not unlawfully interfere with law enforcement. No matter how much you believe in the rightness of your actions, it will not go well.

26. Knowing your rights means understanding when to exercise them.

27. We currently live in a technology society. Your daily WIP should include recording any and all encounters with law enforcement and other authority figures. I am not suggesting that they cannot be trusted, but better safe, than sorry.

---

[19] baptradingcards.com/right-to-counsel-sixth-amendment-and-critical-stages

8 STOP, QUESTION AND FRISK

"Hope is not born, therefore it cannot die."
Vinny Green

It is essential that we take the time to understand the legal definition of an arrest. In the process of a lawful arrest, the individual executing the arrest will be using *legal authority* to deny a person of his or her liberty of movement. An arrest is commonly made with a court-ordered warrant. An arrest might be made without a warrant if, *probable cause*, or what is called, *exigent circumstances*, exist at the time of the arrest.

In the United States justice system, *probable cause* is the legal standard by which law enforcement justifies obtaining an arrest warrant or the issuing of a search warrant. The basis behind the requirement of either of these two actions is to limit those in authority from performing arbitrary or abusive searches, or denial of freedoms, and to encourage lawful evidence gathering during criminal arrest and prosecution.

These controls emanate from the Fourth Amendment of the United States Constitution: *The right of the people to be secure in their persons, houses, papers, and effects, against unreasonable searches and seizures, shall not be violated, and no Warrants shall issue, but upon probable cause, supported by Oath or affirmation, and particularly describing the place to be searched, and the persons or things to be seized*[20].

---

[20] https://www.law.cornell.edu/wex/arrest

An *exigent circumstance*, with respect to the United States criminal procedure requires that under certain circumstances, law enforcement may enter a structure without a search warrant if a situation exists where people are in imminent danger, or there is the possibility of evidence being destroyed, or there exist the possibility of the imminent escape of a suspect.[21]

Law Enforcement may detain an individual if there is *probable cause* or *reasonable suspicion* that a suspect committed; is committing or is about to commit a crime.

Reasonable suspicion is a standard of proof that is less than *probable cause*, which is the legal standard for arrests and warrants, but more than a developing suspicion. Reasonable suspicion must be based on detailed and articulable facts. The suspicion must also be associated with the individual in question at the time[22].

If law enforcement additionally has reasonable suspicion that a person so detained is armed and dangerous, they may "frisk" the person for weapons, or other items that may have the potential to cause harm.

Reasonable suspicion is evaluated using the "reasonable person" or "reasonable officer" standard, in which a person in the same set of circumstances could reasonably suspect a person has been, is, or is about to be engaged in criminal activity.[23]

Allow the law enforcement officer to state the reason for stopping you. Whether the reason is explicitly stated or not, ask if you are under arrest or free to leave.

If you are free to leave, advise the officer that you would like to avail yourself of that option, if that is in fact, what you wish to do[24].

---

[21] https://www.law.cornell.edu/wex/arrest
[22] https://quizlet.com/3037794/criminal-justice-terms-2-flash-cards/
[23] https://www.law.cornell.edu/wex/arrest
[24] https://www.youtube.com/watch?v=vA0ebfV3JRl

Showing Identification

"Stop and identify" statutes are statutory laws in the United States that authorize law enforcement to legally demand the identity of someone whom they reasonably suspect of having committed a crime.

In the United States, interactions between law enforcement and citizens fall into three general categories:

➢ Consensual ("contact" or "conversation"),
➢ Detention (often called a Terry stop, after Terry v. Ohio, 392 U.S. 1 (1968),
➢ Arrest. "Stop and identify" laws pertain to detentions[25].

Without reasonable suspicion that a crime has been committed, is being committed, or about to be committed, an individual is not required to provide identification, even in "Stop and ID" states.

A different set of obligations apply to individuals operating motor vehicles. These individuals are usually required by state motor vehicle laws to present a driver's license to law enforcement when requested.

The Fourth Amendment to the United States Constitution's bans unreasonable searches and seizures. The amendment demands a warrant to be Court-ordered and that the standard of probable cause be met.

In the Supreme Court case of Terry v. Ohio, 392 U.S. 1 (1968), it was ruled to be constitutionally acceptable for law enforcement to temporarily detain an individual based on an articulable reasonable suspicion that a crime has been committed, and to conduct a "pat-down" if there be a reasonable belief that the individual may be armed.

---

[25] https://en.wikipedia.org/wiki/Stop_and_identify_statutes

The question whether or not it is permissible for law enforcement to demand that a person being detained provide his or her name was considered by the Court in Hiibel v. Sixth Judicial District Court of Nevada, 542 U.S. 177 (2004). In the Hiibel case, the court maintained that the name disclosure did not violate the Fourth Amendment prohibition on unreasonable searches and seizures[26].

The Hiibel case also held that, because the defendant, Hiibel, had no reasonable belief that his name would be used to incriminate himself, the name disclosure did not violate his Fifth Amendment right against self-incrimination.

However, the Court left open the possibility that an individual's Fifth Amendment right might apply in situations where there was a reasonable belief that giving a name could be incriminating.

As of February 2011, there is no U.S. federal law requiring that individuals identify themselves during a *Terry* stop, but *Hiibel* held that states might enact such laws, provided the law require the officer to have reasonable and articulable suspicion of criminal involvement. As of the abovementioned date, the validity of a law requiring that a person detained provide anything more than stating his or her name has not come before the U.S. Supreme Court.[27]

Further information concerning state-by-state requirements with respect to the showing of identification may be found at https://en.wikipedia.org/wiki/Stop_and_identify_statutes

---

[26] https://en.wikipedia.org/wiki/Stop_and_identify_statutes
[27] https://en.wikipedia.org/wiki/Stop_and_identify_statutes

9 VEHICLE STOPS

"People don't lose Hope; they chose to leave it behind."
Vinny Green

There are several lawful rationales for why law enforcement might conduct a traffic stop. One of the most frequently utilized forms of stops would be, Driving Under the Influence, also known as a DUI checkpoint. These checkpoints are largely meant to detect drivers who may be operating a motor vehicle while under the influence of alcohol or drugs.

Every day, roughly, 30 people in the United States perish in drunk-driving collisions—this translated into one person every 48 minutes in 2017. While these deaths have fallen by a third in the last three decades, due mainly to enforcement actions, the reality is that drunk driving crashes claim more than 10,000 lives per year[28]. Keep in mind that this number does not speak to the thousands who are injured and often disabled in these events.

Drunk driving is a topic that G-Square extensively discusses in our Defensive Driving Courses. The compiled statistic of 10,000 deaths alone, do not even come close to addressing the big picture.

Each death represents a family, not just an individual. If we can safely assume that each family conservatively consists of four people, this means that 10,000 deaths, at a minimum, impact 40,000

---

[28] https://www.nhtsa.gov/risky-driving/drunk-driving

people. All of this has a ripple effect that cannot be easily calculated.

Statistics such as these scream for some type of rule enforcement to be in place to work at protecting the public, and generations to come. In most societies, this has fallen on the shoulders of law enforcement to be responsible for protecting the people and the future. Unfortunately, these stops far too often result in the incarceration of the driver and sometimes the vehicle occupants, and sadly, sometimes an individual's death; this cannot continue.

Drivers must understand their rights in a DUI stop and be prepared to comply with the requirements that come with the privilege of operating a motor vehicle. We must also understand that driving is not a right. Driving is in fact, a privilege, which has the possibility of a negative outcome that may materialize when stopped by members of law enforcement for violating one or more of the rules that come with this privilege.

According to the National Highway Traffic Safety Administration (NHTSA), about 1.5 million people are arrested in a given year for driving under the influence of alcohol or drugs. That statistic means that one out of every 121 licensed drivers were arrested for drunk driving.

The NHTSA also reports that automobile collisions are the number one cause of death in young adults age 15-20. Statistics also show that of these fatal collisions, 28 percent involved alcohol consumption[29].

If a driver is believed to be operating a vehicle while impaired due to being under the influence of alcohol, drugs or any substances that may impair judgment or an individual's ability to safely operate a vehicle, that individual when stopped is likely to be asked to take a blood-alcohol and/or coordination test.

---

[29] http://www.drunkdrivingprevention.com/index.html

Close Encounters of the Law Enforcement Kind

What we each must recognize, and in many cases come to terms with, is that in obtaining a driver's license it comes with what is called "implied consent," which means the possibility of taking these tests. The imposed penalty for refusing a blood alcohol test in many states' rests on the principle of implied consent.

Implied consent means that by using the public roads, you have consented to safe chemical testing or blood alcohol tests. In addition, implied consent means that in earning a driver's license, the individual has given consent to take these tests when a professional law enforcement officer determines the situation is appropriate.

If the driver of the vehicle fails the tests or refuses to take the test, many states will allow a law enforcement officer to effect an arrest of the individual. In so doing, the individual's driver's license may be suspended, and vehicle impounded. If arrested, it is likely that the vehicle being driven will be subject to a search.

In the interest of safety, expediency, and cooperation, upon request, show law enforcement a valid driver's license, vehicle registration, and proof of car insurance.

Think about it; a driver has been issued these documents for that reason; as offers of proof that they can legally operate a motor vehicle, and that the motor vehicle in question is properly registered and insured. Who else would a driver feel comfortable in showing these documents, if not a person with the lawful authority to request and review them?

Please, have these items in a place that is a short visible reach. As a safety precaution, do not reach for any of these documents without first advising law enforcement what is being reached for and where it is in the vehicle.

Again, never engage in an action where hands are not visible when dealing with law enforcement. Standard training for law enforcement includes making sure, that an officer can always see the hands of an individual the officer is encountering. The reasoning behind this training theory is that if the officer is going to be injured,

Close Encounters of the Law Enforcement Kind

it will be done by something in the person's hands.

Any well-trained officer is always going to be sensitive to what is in someone's hands or reachable by an individual's hands. I am not asking anyone to agree with this thought process; I am providing this information as a statement of fact. Please keep this in mind.

In certain cases, an individual's vehicle can be searched without a warrant. No matter what documents are presented, it is recommended that the operator or owner of the vehicle make it clear that consent is not given to search the vehicle. Just make the statement for the record. We do not suggest that any attempt is made to physically stop the search.

DUI checkpoints are one of the most common traffic stops used by law enforcement, resulting in a significant number of arrests annually.

While most people think of DUI checkpoints in terms of being a method of reducing drunk driving, and they do play a large part in that goal; these procedures also function as an opportunity where law enforcement may take the occasion to get a close look into a vehicle by briefly detaining a motorist.

A DUI stop is usually quick, but it allows law enforcement an opportunity to check the occupant's license and registration. It also provides an officer with an opportunity to take a quick whiff of the driver's breath to see if he or she may have consumed alcohol. It also grants the officer a chance to see into the vehicle to observe for any suspicious items in plain sight.

Your constitutional rights do not take a day off. Those rights also apply in these types of situations. While legally, these types of stops are permitted, law enforcement is not permitted to search you or your vehicle without probable cause that you are under the influence or you agree to the search.

10 IF LAW ENFORCEMENT COMES TO YOUR HOME

"We are not byproducts of our environment.
We are the products of our choices to our environment."
Vinny Green

Law enforcement can enter your home without your permission if they have a warrant, or if it is an emergency. If law enforcement says they have a warrant, it is recommended that you request to see the warrant.

To begin with, check to make sure the warrant has the correct address. Pay attention to such things as street, avenue, road, and/or apartment number. It is not unusual for this type of information to be entered incorrectly, misread, or sometimes, an informant or other source has provided the wrong information to law enforcement.

If you detect an error, bring it to the attention of the law enforcement officer. As in all situations, it is recommended that you contact a criminal defense attorney.

If arrested in your home or office, law enforcement can search you and the area immediately surrounding you. The search can include where evidence of criminal activity or grabbable items that could cause potential harm to the officer or a third party are present. The search can also include objects that are in plain view.

It is understood that recent developments in the news, or possibly in your life, might have you intimidated at the thought of an encounter with law enforcement, especially when an officer is knocking on your door or pulling you over.

47

Close Encounters of the Law Enforcement Kind

To be honest, I have been a law enforcement officer for forty years and have more experience than most any officer that may approach me, but I too become concerned when approached by a law enforcement officer.

As already stated, the majority of law enforcement officers have one goal, and only one goal, to serve the people. Believe it or not, that includes you. Like any other public servant, officers are trained and required to follow established rules, regulations, and laws.

As a member of the public, it is to your advantage to become familiar with as many of these rules and laws as possible. Doing so will help protect your rights and avoid negative encounters with professional members of law enforcement.

No Warrant, No Search!

The Supreme Court of the United States has ruled that a person's home is entitled to protection from unreasonable search and seizure. Even if an officer has probable cause to believe something illegal is taking place inside of your dwelling, in most cases, he or she must obtain a signed warrant before entering the home without permission.

As Supreme Court rulings currently stand, the only exception to the search warrant requirement would be if an officer requests permission to enter the home and *consent* were given by someone with authority to grant access.

Consent is something that should be given careful thought before granting to law enforcement. If an officer is legally invited into a dwelling, you would be subject to the "Plain Sight" or "Plain View" Doctrine." Plain View is a doctrine that supports that when an officer is given consent to enter a dwelling or is in the dwelling by virtue of a legally signed warrant, that any illegal items that are out in the open or in "plain view" can be seized as evidence, and ultimately used in a prosecutorial proceeding.

Close Encounters of the Law Enforcement Kind

Why are you knocking on my door?

While having a law enforcement officer knock on your door may not be the norm, it is probably in your interest to treat the arrival the same way that you would handle any other unanticipated visitor. The best course of action, as with any encounter with law enforcement is to first, stay calm and respectful. Follow this with a request of, "How may I help you, officer."

Many times, the reason for the visit may have nothing to do with you. The officers may be seeking information that you can help them in obtaining. Taking a hostile stance to the intended statement of, I would like your help, could thrust this encounter into a downward encounter that need not happen.

An officer may be seeking information about a crime committed nearby or some other situation that you may be able to help in resolving by answering a question or two.

If the officer is there investigating a crime that may have taken place in your home or one in which you are thought to have been involved, continue with the repeated recommendation throughout this publication. Exercise your right to remain silent and obtain competent legal counsel. Advise the officer that without a signed warrant, you do not think it is in your best interest to allow the officer into your home.

As it is likely that not everyone that you know will be privy to this advice, we recommend that you share these recommendations with friends, relatives, and roommates.

Take the time to caution them not to give consent to allow law enforcement to enter your room or domicile that you may be sharing, or even if they are just visiting and happen to answer a knock on the door that turns out to be law enforcement.

These recommendations are not formed or presented as a means to hide illegal activity. We do not support, in any way, the idea of using loopholes or other opportunities for individuals engaging in criminal activity or those providing Aid and Abet for criminals to escape justice. These recommendations are presented to educate the law-abiding citizen of his or her constitutional rights.

With respect to roommates, college students should be sensitive to their rights when occupying a dormitory room, with or without a roommate.

Students must recognize that moving into a dormitory setting comes with the abdication of many of the rights to privacy that are enjoyed living at home.

Your home is just that, your home, which you control. In most cases, occupying a dormitory room comes with implied consent that you agree to follow the college's rules concerning access to the room. Make sure you are aware of the level of consent that comes with occupancy.

With the rental of an apartment comes certain rights. Dorm rooms are the property of the school and do not necessarily come with the same rights as a Landlord/Tenant arrangement.

With ownership by the college, you will find school officials and campus security acting on the school's behalf exercising a level of control at which they feel entitled with respect to entering rooms occupied by enrolled students.

Many students do not give this much thought. However, being familiar with and respectfully exercising your rights is a level of protection that each student should feel comfortable engaging in on campus, the same way they would do elsewhere.

The United States Supreme Court has ruled that an occupant of a residence *can* refuse consent, even if other roommates agree to a search. You must be present in order to assert this refusal. With these rules in place, it is important to make sure that all occupants understand their 4th Amendment rights in case something happens when you are not around. You may want to talk to your roommates about how to handle visits from law enforcement.

Close Encounters of the Law Enforcement Kind

In general, law enforcement can gain consent to search from anyone with control over the property. Someone who has a key, or whose name appears on the lease, can legally consent to a search of the property if no one else is present, or if no one else objects.

Securing your space can help protect you if a roommate decides to grant access to law enforcement without your consent. If your room is off-limits to your roommates and their friends, courts will often rule that it is off-limits to law enforcement without a warrant, as well.

11 IF YOU ARE TAKEN INTO CUSTODY

"There is never a need to repackage the truth; it comes ready to eat."

Vinny Green

You have the right to remain silent. It is recommended that you exercise that right. Do not discuss any particulars of the matter you are being arrested or detained for with anyone until you have obtained competent criminal legal counsel.

It is also recommended that you only provide pedigree information, unless your criminal attorney is present, or has given you direction to do otherwise.

It is suggested that you do not give any explanations, excuses, or stories. You can make your defense later, in court, based on what you and your criminal lawyer decides is the best course of action.

If you have a lawyer, ask to speak with your lawyer immediately. If you are unable to afford a lawyer, you have the right to have a lawyer assigned to you at no cost once your case reaches a **critical** stage, as discussed in chapter four. Refrain from speaking about your situation to anyone until that appointment happens.

If you are uncertain as to how to contact a criminal attorney, you are entirely within your rights to ask law enforcement how to contact the Public Defender's Office.

It is strongly recommended that you locate a criminal attorney now and keep his or her contact information with you at all times, you just never know when legal services are going to be needed, remember WIP.

Within a reasonable time after you are detained, you should ask to make contact with a family member; friend or someone that you are comfortable will act in your best interest.

If you are permitted to make a call, do not assume that your conversations are not being overheard by law enforcement or others in custody. It would not be in your best interest to discuss the facts of your case over the phone. It is advised that you not make decisions on your case, sign any documents, or make statements without having consulted with a competent criminal attorney.

CONCLUSION

"It is not enough to give the message; you must also be the message."
Vinny Green

Early in my career, I developed a passion for improving the lives of everyone with whom I share the air. I awake each day, confident that there is a better way. Confident that there is a better me.

With that in mind, I begin each day, and I conclude most writings by thanking the Lord for the blessing of being me, and I ask for the inner strength and wisdom to continue being a model and not a critic.

Some years ago, I heard motivational speaker Les Brown end one of his presentations with the following words, which I begin each day with as my call to begin each day as a light and not a judge:

If you want something bad enough, go out and fight for it.

Work day and night for it.

Give up your time, your peace, and your sleep for it.

If all that you dream, and scheme is about it, and life seems useless and worthless without it.

If you will gladly sweat for it, fret for it, plan for it, and lose all terror of the opposition for it.

If you simply go after that thing that you want with all your capacity, strength and sagacity, faith, hope, and confidence and stern pertinacity.

Close Encounters of the Law Enforcement Kind

If neither cold, poverty, famine nor gout, sickness nor pain of body or brain can keep you away from that thing that you want.

If dogged and grim, you besiege and beset it. With the help of God, you will get it![30]

CARPE DIEM!

---

[30]https://www.linkedin.com/pulse/you-want-thing-bad-enough-les-brown-andre-rynhardt-barnard

QUIZ ANSWERS
KNOW YOUR RIGHTS!

DO YOU KNOW WHAT YOU THINK YOU KNOW?

1. **Can a male officer search a female?** *There is no law that prohibits a male officer from searching a female suspect or a female from searching a male. This information does not mean that various department policies might not prohibit such actions.*

2. **When arrested, must an individual be immediately read Miranda Warnings?** *Miranda is not required unless the suspect is being questioned about the conduct, which he or she is being arrested.*

3. **Is law enforcement allowed to lie during an interview or interrogation?** *Yes, within certain limitations*

4. **When do constitutional rights to counsel attach?**

    A person's right to counsel indelibly attaches to a matter upon any one of three triggering events

    > *(1) Entry or retaining of counsel on the matter.*

    > *(2) Commencement of a criminal prosecution of the matter.*

    > *(3) Request for counsel or invocation of the right to counsel concerning the matter while held in custody.* [31]

5. **Who is your city council member or equivalent?** *This individual can be of help during these encounters.*

6. **Who is your state senator or equivalent?** *This individual can be of help during these encounters.*

7. **Who is your assemblyperson or equivalent?** *This individual can be of help during these encounters.*

---

[31] https://www.newyorkappellatelawyer.com/right-to-counsel-constitutional-rules/

8.   **Who is your lawyer versed in criminal matters?** *If you do not have a criminal lawyer, get one. It is better to have one and not need one; than to need one and not have him.*

G-SQUARE INTERNATIONAL TRAINING ACADEMY

WWW.G-SQUARE.ORG

GSCTraining@optimum.net

(917) 681-2810

Made in the USA
Middletown, DE
30 April 2021